Finding
The
Way

Finding
The
Way

Selections from the Writings of
DALE EVANS ROGERS

Fleming H. Revell Company
Old Tappan, New Jersey

All Scripture quotations in this volume are from the King James Version of the Bible.

Acknowledgement is made for use of material from the following books copyrighted by Fleming H. Revell Company: Angel Unaware, copyright 1953; My Spiritual Diary, copyright 1955; To My Son, copyright 1957; Christmas Is Always, copyright © 1958; No Two Ways About It! copyright © 1963; Dearest Debbie, copyright © 1965; Time Out, Ladies! copyright © 1966; Salute To Sandy, copyright 1967; The Woman At the Well, copyright © 1970; Cool It Or Lose It! copyright © 1972.

Library of Congress Cataloging in Publication Data

Rogers, Dale Evans.
    Finding the way.
    Published in 1969 under title: God has the answers.
    1. Meditations.   I. Title.
BV4832.2 1973   248'.3   73-3356
ISBN 0-8007-0604-8

Finding
The
Way

I do not want to pose as one who has all the answers; the longer I live the more I realize how little I know. . . . Christ, not I, has the answers. He is *the* answer to every human need. I speak not out of any vain authority of my own, but only for His authority, for in every crisis in my life I have found Him able to do for me what I could not do for myself. . . .

When I turned thirty, I thought, "Well, I may as well go pick out my shroud. . . ." Nothing "worked" for me in those days, because I wouldn't let the Lord work His way in my heart.

I know whereof I speak, for I have been through it—through hasty, ill-considered, un-Christian marriage, disillusionment, separation, divorce—but thanks be to God, He finally got through to me, and my heart had its hardness taken away, and my life transformed, and I have known the joy of *a real* marriage. I know now that divorce settles nothing, but that God binding the hearts of man and wife together can settle *anything*.

. . . How I wish I'd had spiritual strength and trust in God at the time of my first marriage. Had I been a true Christian then, I would never have had to face that dismal experience of divorce. But my son's father wanted his freedom, and my pride was hurt, and so it happened.

Then, when I reached thirty-five, Christ came into my life, and . . . now it does work and nothing is so important as the "now." *Now* is all we really have— not yesterday, nor tomorrow, but now. ". . . now is the accepted time . . . now is the day of salvation" (II CORINTHIANS 6:2). It is never too late to make a marriage work, to turn to Christ to be forgiven and strengthened, and to start again.

We rush through life so fast that we don't even know the flowers are there.

But it doesn't have to be like this. You can decide to do otherwise, to travel another way. This is *your* life. Choose ye this day. . . .

Now sooner or later in this life, like the man on the road to Jericho, we all discover that there are thieves lying in wait for us to rob us of our chance to really *live.* There are good values and bad values screaming for our money and/or our lives; there is God and the devil, and we will eventually travel with one or the other. You can't avoid it: you will have to choose between them. God cannot and will not do it for you. He gives you your years, your breath of life; you can use it either for Him or against Him.

Since I have come to know God and walk His way, the pressures and temptations that made my life so empty before I knew Him have disappeared completely. His power makes my life abundant instead of merely successful. He would do the same for you.

How did we come to decide that money and not God, not Christ, is *power?* . . . Jesus never said that money was evil *in itself.* What He said was that our misdirected *love* of money was the *root* of all evil. I think Jesus believed in free enterprise; His parable of the talents indicates that to me. I believe He expected us to use our God-given talents to make as good a living as we can, to acquire and use our possessions well, *but never to make possessions the great goal of life.* . . .

The Bible says that any man who says he loves God but hates his fellow man is a liar; we could change that to say that we hate God when we push Him aside to grab that buck. We are like the rich old rascal who had stolen a fortune in his lifetime and who sent for the preacher, to be baptized, when he was dying. After the ceremony the preacher said to him, "Well, brother, if you had your life to live over again, do you think you would do better?" The old man replied, "Frankly, parson, I think I've done pretty darned well, as it is!"

Do you want that, or do you want the spiritual wealth of the One who died on a cross possessed of only one torn, seamless robe?

I have often wished that children might bring with them, when they are born, a prenatal instruction in the dictum laid down by Paul in EPHESIANS 6:1—"Children, obey your parents. . . ." Insofar as we know, Paul had no children, but he sure knew what he was talking about when he said *that!* "Children, obey your parents, *in the Lord*. . . ." The Lord is the Creator of parents, and He meant them to be obeyed, but as I look around me I think not only the children, but many of the parents as well, either do not know of this Pauline counsel, or deliberately ignore it if they do. Obedience seems to be something that passed out with the one-hoss shay and kerosene lamps—something our fathers and mothers knew, but passé and old-fashioned now. Some "child experts" tell mothers that they must not "inhibit" their children by forcing them to do *anything*. All due credit to them, I think these expert child psychologists and "liberal" educators have done us a great disservice and a lot of harm. . . . I plead guilty to an occasional retreat into the "Oh, well" philosophy, and I have always found it a rough road to travel, later on. God says "No" to us many, many times in life. He has been saying it for centuries. When a thing is wrong, He shouts "No!" and if we disobey, we pay for it. It never fails.

Let's *mean* "No" when we say "No." *But let us say it in love,* never in frustration or in a fit of uncontrolled temper. I have just quoted Paul, in EPHESIANS 6. Let me quote him again, in the same chapter: "And, ye fathers [he might have said 'Mothers'], provoke not your children to wrath . . ." (v. 4). Try to understand their problems before you reach for the hairbrush. Their problems are as important to them as ours are to us.

Why are we all so anxious to keep up with the Joneses and not at all anxious to keep in touch with God? Why, in this rat race, do we become the abject slaves of people who design everything in our lives for us, from morals to hats, from houses to hairdos? I plead guilty to yielding to their pressure too often.

But my Bible tells me that God expects me to stand before Him with clean hands and a pure heart (read the Twenty-fourth Psalm). He demands that I—we—stand up and be counted, and we must set that divine demand against the demand of the world to cheapen our characters for the sake of top billing in our jobs. Long ago, Roy and I had to face this, and we made a decision about it. In his early days as a Western star, Roy insisted that he would play only clean, wholesome parts. . . .

We took a stand, and if it cost us that much in the movies it didn't cost as much, for God has opened other careers to us in which we are not pressured into such decisions. . . .

The Christian in show business or anywhere else has his trials and tribulations; Christ never promised

him that he would have no trials and tribulations, but He did promise help in conquering them. Those who scoff at God and turn from Him may think they're winning, but they're duped. When they come to the end of their earthly success—what then?—even though they die in a palace?

Have you ever stopped to think of what you would do if God were to tell you that you had just one more day to live? Someone asked St. Francis about that, and he replied, "I would go on hoeing my garden." I like that. I like starting the day with God in prayer and meditation. It's a good idea to do what the old-fashioned preacher said he did when he was asked the secret of his good preaching; he said, "I just stay prayed up."

We have a firm morning schedule in our house. . . . After the last slam of the door, Mama sits down to a cup of coffee and surveys her echoing domain. It's time now for her to read some Scripture, to think a moment on her blessings, and to ask God's help for the long day ahead. I wouldn't dream of starting the day without that; I couldn't get through the rest of the day without it. I have long since learned to take one day at a time, to take one step at a time and trust God for the next, and to know that without God all through my day, I might not have tomorrow.

After devotional time I try to snatch a few minutes for a walk up the mountain behind our house, to "the rock." It's *my* rock, and God's; He put it there for me to enjoy. It is a big stone, flat on the top, overlooking Chatsworth Lake. On clear days, I can see for miles in every direction from my rock, and sometimes I just sit there drinking in the beauty all around, feeling my heart grow warm with gratitude for the goodness of the God who created it. Other times, I stretch out flat on the rock, close my eyes and let Him clear away the confusion of my mind and let the warmth of the sun sink into me. I try to think of nothing in particular, but simply wait for the still, small voice to speak. . . .

I have another "quiet spot" in addition to my rock; my altar and chapel. A friend of mine gave me an old-fashioned kneeling bench, and many a time, when the pressure becomes almost more than I can bear, that hallowed little altar has been a place of refuge and a re-fueling station. I use it when I haven't time to climb up to my rock. I always find God there, waiting for me to come. He will always be there, always at the little altar, and it strengthens me to know that. Of course, the whole house is His—but that little altar and kneeling bench are especially set aside for Him, and for me, and for our quiet communion together. Do you have an altar in your house? You could—just one corner that is dedicated to God, where His book is always open.

This status business gives me a pain!

We blunder on, refusing to be extreme, or *definite*, about our convictions and our moral standards. It might offend someone, or some group. It might affect our incomes or—perish the thought!—our "status." What was the status of Jesus Christ in Palestinian society? How much did He have in the bank when He died? Just which group in Jerusalem did He tell His followers was "important" enough for Him to "cultivate"?

Then there is sex.

You can't escape sex; you've got it, and that's that. I don't see any reason why we should want to escape it, or run away from it. I don't particularly object to a boy knowing he's a boy, or a girl knowing she's different from a boy; what I do object to is giving the boy or girl the gutter version or outlook on sex. . . .

God gave us sex, as He gave us all else, and He never meant it to be what we have made of it in the name of "realism."

But some authors and playwrights use that word "realism" as a blanket excuse for a flood of suggestive and obscene words, language that would disgrace a community of Hottentots, to say nothing of a decent American community. . . .

My Bible says of the marriage relation, "Therefore shall a man leave his father and mother, and shall cleave unto his wife: and they shall be one flesh." God meant it to be like that; He never meant it to be a gimmick for lewd entertainment.

We have a Hollywood Christian Group that meets every Monday night. Anyone in show business is eligible for membership. Our aim is to introduce our fellow workers to Jesus Christ, to hope that they will accept Him as Guide and Lord of their lives and then go out and witness to others. We started with high hopes that this Christian effort might be effective against the money-success-sex-crime pressures being brought against the public. We hoped that young, ambitious actors and actresses might become so firmly grounded in the gospel through the group that they would turn down degrading roles even at the sacrifice of quick success.

. . . Too many evaded it. That isn't the fault of the gospel, or of Jesus Christ. When any Christian stalls on such a decision, it is *his* fault. It is "the lust of the flesh, and the lust of the eyes, and the pride of life" that does it—that "does him in." It is not God but Satan who tempts us to eat the forbidden fruit.

But some do accept the challenge, and take the dare. Let me tell you about one girl who did.

Bonnie came to work with us as an extra, in one of

our TV pictures. . . . One afternoon, during a lull in the shooting, she came over to me and asked, "What is that you are reading—a *Bible?*" Her voice was loaded with incredulity; she just couldn't believe it. We talked awhile, and I invited her to the next meeting of the Hollywood Christian Group. She came, she listened, and the incredulity drained from her; she said, "I like it. I'll come back, as soon as I get out of the hospital."

I was shocked to learn she had a lump in her breast, but Bonnie laughed at me, "I'm not worried about it," she said.

The day after her operation, Bonnie's mother phoned to say that her daughter had asked for me. As soon as the day's work was over, I went. The operation had been quite extensive; the growth was definitely malignant. She asked me to repeat the Twenty-Third Psalm for her, which I did. We talked about the Good Shepherd and it came clearly to her that the Shepherd loved her and wanted her heart and wanted to give her eternal life. She put her hand in mine, and in that gesture put it also into the hand of God. She prayed a halting, choking little prayer, asking forgiveness and acceptance. She was smiling when I left the room—a smile, I was to discover, that even death could not take from her pain-tortured face.

We were very close friends, after that. Together we watched the inevitable progress of the cancer. We prayed together through three long years of radium treatments, hysterectomy, cobalt, in-and-out of the hospital. We prayed that she might be healed and we prayed for strength when it became clearly evident that the case was terminal. One day she asked pitifully, "Dale, why doesn't God heal me?" I couldn't give her the answer I longed to give—that God *would* heal her—but she understood when I told her that we must rest on God's promise that "all things work together for good to them that love God, to them who are the called according to his purpose." She accepted that, and prayed on, and kept coming to the Group meetings. Toward the last, when the cancer had reached through the bloodstream into her whole body, she hobbled to our meetings on crutches.

With a friend I stood at her bedside, appalled at the wasting-away of her body, but inspired beyond words by the beauty and brilliance of her shining eyes. Her courage was beyond anything I had ever seen.

She had one frightful spell I'll never forget, but when she came out of it she pointed toward the ceiling and said, "Look. Look up there. The light: it's so white and shining. It's the Lord—the beauty and the glory of the Lord. Can't you see it?" Her head rolled and the heavy eyelids twitched, and just before the merciful coma came she whispered, "Dale, it's so beautiful. I'm going up there, to be at home with God." The following week, the phone rang and her mother told me that our little "extra" had gone home.

Bonnie's name was never up in lights or headlines. Yes, she died an extra playing minor roles, as Hollywood thinks of roles, but in the eyes of God she had won top billing in the Kingdom, and I know of no other success worth mentioning.

I say she won. I say the laurels God gave her made the laurels men give look like poisonous weeds. I say the light and glamour which surrounded her make the glamour of this world look like darkness.

Christ said, "My peace I give unto you: not as the world giveth, give I unto you. . . ." and "Lo, I am with you always, even unto the end. . . ."

The more *things* you have, the more you want. They can never satisfy, never bring the happiness you have reached for and missed. Only the peace of God in your heart can bring you that.

Success doesn't do it, either. I know of more than one highly successful man and woman who would be better off dead. Success can cost too much; most of us can't afford it. Jesus warned us that we can lose our souls getting it—and if you lose your soul, what's left? All this contains no satisfying answer because God is not in it—*and because God Himself is the answer.*

If we haven't God's map to guide us, we'll get lost, or crack up—and fast. . . .

The Bible is God's map in the hands of men. . . . It is a map that describes a road as old as time, a road older than history, starting in Eden with two sinners running and terrified.

On this road is every pain and problem known to man, and every peril of life. And for every pain and problem there is an answer and a relief, from the map called the Bible. For every stumbling block there is a warning, for every sickness a cure, and strength, always, to go on. Man has provided stumbling blocks for every mile, but on every inch of the road is the outstretched hand of God.

It is a beautiful map; the greatest writers bow to it and despair of ever writing anything equal to it. It is a *true* map; it never lies and it will not lead you astray; it is not myth nor fable nor fairy tale. It is as

real as your breath. It is filled with people who face
the same problems that you face on the road and they
are put in the Bible so that you can see what happened to them when they traveled with God, and
without Him; you can profit thereby, and stumble
less often.

It's quite a map. If there is a better one for us to
travel by, I haven't seen it. No other map from any
other who ever lived offers me and you such a sure
guide to abundant life on earth, and in heaven too.

Why do we have so much juvenile crime and de-
linquency? It's as plain as the nose on your face. Our
children are given no moral or spiritual guidance in
the school; family prayers have all but disappeared in
the large majority of our homes, and many a child
never enters a church or church school for the simple
reason that their *parents* never enter them. When I
went to school as a child in Osceola, Arkansas, we re-
cited the Lord's Prayer in the classroom every morning, and on Fridays we had "chapel," with singing,
Bible reading, prayer, and a minister from a different
church to talk to us. I loved it, and all my schoolmates

loved it; I have yet to hear of one of them saying it did him or her any harm. I was fortunate to have it like that—and fortunate to have the teaching continued in a home in which Bible-loving and church-going parents took up where the school left off. I pity the youngsters who do not have this today. . . .

Jesus Christ said, ". . . ye shall know the truth, and the truth shall make you free" (JOHN 8:32). What's wrong with a child knowing His truth? He declared, "I am the way, the truth, and the life . . ." (JOHN 14:6). Why should a child be denied all the knowledge he can get about that Way and that life? Is it *sinful* to give him that? Jesus said, when He departed from the earth, He would send the Comforter, the Holy Spirit, to guide us into all truth. And how do we go about contacting this Holy Spirit, so that we may be guided to the truth? We do it through honest, constant, sincere prayer, in invoking the Spirit through communion with Him. We do it through the Guide Book we call the Bible—and we can never read enough or think enough about that Bible, in school or home or church or anywhere else. If the God of the Book becomes no longer our Supreme Authority in the affairs of men and nations, then what, or who, *is* the authority?

Are *people,* with all their confusions and conflicts

and clashing opinions and differing interpretations, to be the final authority? Did you ever see two people who agreed on anything, down to the smallest detail? People must have a *standard* to live by if they want to live in peace, and not like beasts in the jungle. When a country goes off her economic standard, there is economic confusion. Right? When people desert their tried and tested moral standards, there is moral chaos. Right? And when we desert the religious standards that are warp and woof of our great country, and that have made us the great power we are in the family of nations—well, what then?

Don't *we* dare protest against *anything* anymore?

When I was ten years old, I accepted Christ as my Saviour. I was given a Bible and told to read it regularly and carefully, and that if I did I would find help and guidance and I would live the kind of life God wanted me to live. But there was a lot of competition for that Bible, and the competition won. I read it regularly for awhile, then I began to skip a day every now and then. I gradually stopped praying every day, too, probably because I didn't get everything I asked for. I began to take detours off the main road, and I got myself into all kinds of trouble simply because I wasn't following His holy Word.

This term, "The Word," fascinates me. It's been in our religion from the start. In the very first verse of John's Gospel, "In the beginning was the Word, and the Word was with God, and the Word was God." God spoke that Word into the hearts of certain men He chose to represent Him on earth—men like Moses, David, Isaiah, Jeremiah, Ezekiel and the other prophets of the Old Testament; the Word was a form of divine revelation, it was the way God told men the truth about Himself, and made Himself clear to them. In another sense, the Word is the Scriptures—the Bible. Someone has described the Bible as "man's attempt to find God." I think it may also be a record of God's attempt to find man and guide him.

It is God calling to us as we walk the earthly way, telling us which way to turn, how to avoid the stumbling blocks and the thieves who lie in wait. . . .

Then "the Word was made flesh, and dwelt among us, [and we beheld his glory, the glory as of the only begotten of the Father], full of grace and truth." This was Jesus Christ, the Word in the flesh of a Man, sent as a Guide for the road, sent that we might know what God was really like, and that He was always with us on the road. Christ is God pointing the way through this life and the way beyond; in Christ the Word becomes a map reaching past the horizon to *eternal* life. The Word was crucified on Calvary that we who accept Him and that sacrifice might walk with Him in life everlasting.

There is constant evidence that our *children*, generally speaking, are not as well acquainted with the Bible as they are with Mickey Mouse and Little Red Riding Hood. That isn't their fault; it's ours. It's supposed to be funny to hear the children display their ignorance of the Book of books—like the little girl who told Art Linkletter that Alice in Wonderland was her favorite Bible story, or the boy who answered, in a quiz, the question "What are the Epistles?" by saying that the Epistles were the wives of the Apostles. It isn't funny, McGee, it's tragic. . . .

From Plymouth Rock to Virginia, the Bible was planted by our forefathers as the seed of American democracy and a new way of life on a new continent; its precepts are written into the Constitution, creeds, and customs of our land. It is good history—good

American history. If we want our children to love and appreciate America, we had better show them early in their lives that its greatness and freedom are Bible-born.

Listen to U. S. Grant: "The Bible is the sheet anchor of our liberties." Or to Andrew Jackson: "That Book, sir, is the rock upon which our republic rests." Patrick Henry, a rather familiar figure in the fight for American freedom, said that "The Bible is worth more than all the other books that have ever been printed." Abraham Lincoln believed it to be "the greatest gift God has ever given to men." George Washington, who knew something about government, held that it was impossible "rightly to govern the world without God and the Bible." Horace Greeley thought the Bible was responsible for the rise of the common man, and the defense of his rights, in America; he said, "It is impossible to enslave mentally or socially a Bible-reading people. The principles of the Bible are the groundwork of human freedom. . . ."

It's good reading as well as good history—and yet, if this were *all* it is, it wouldn't mean too much to me. It wasn't written to be read as "good literature"; it was written to guide men to God, to lift them from sin and ugly living into abundant life built on the model of the Master. I read in a magazine the other day these arresting words by an unknown author: "The Bible, God's Holy Word, is not to be read like any other book, or like a newspaper, or a magazine; too many blessings are lost unless it is read as a personal message from God Himself." That's it! *That is why we should read it.* You wouldn't refuse to read a letter from your best friend, would you? And if God be your Best Friend, and has something to say to you—?

Some cynics love to point to "the disreputable characters of the Bible." They make me laugh. Certainly some of the Bible folk are disreputable. If Ananias lies, the Bible *calls* him a liar; if a man is a thief or a murderer, the Bible gives him no halo. The Bible does not lie. The people of the Bible are the exhibits of God saying "Beware!" or "This way!" Time and again some fool has tried to destroy it (there was Hitler, remember, and Khrushchev), only to find himself destroyed. Every so often some "scholar" announces funeral services for the Bible, but the "corpse" has an embarrassing way of getting up and walking off, and the funeral has to be postponed. "Heaven and earth shall pass away, but my words shall not pass away," said Jesus Christ.

Father Vincent McNab, an English clergyman, had a friend who knew the daughter of Karl Marx—who was no praying man, by any standard. He says that the two of them one day got to talking about religion, and the daughter of the father of Socialism said, "I was brought up without any religion. I do not believe in God." Then she added wistfully, "But just the other day, in an old German book, I came across a German prayer, and if the God of that prayer exists, I think I could believe in Him." She didn't know the name of the prayer, or anything about its background, but she knew that it began with the words, "Our Father which art in heaven, Hallowed be Thy name. Thy kingdom come. Thy will be done in earth, as it is in heaven" . . . is enough for me.

Our Father which art in heaven. . . . That word "Father" brings Him close—as close as, or closer than, our earthly parents. He is Father of a family—the whole great human family—Father of *all* of us. The word breaks down barriers between us. We are all His creation, all potential sons and heirs of His Kingdom and love. That one word, Father, makes the world a brotherhood. Are you one of those who feel that "God is so far away . . ."? Or that He seems "so formal and cold"? That just isn't true! When you come to see God as a Father, there is a close, intimate relationship with Him. . . .

Dr. Armin C. Oldsen, who speaks over the Lutheran Hour broadcast, asks some pertinent questions about all this: "Is a good father strong? God is perfect strength. Is a good father wise? God is perfect wisdom. Is a good father loving? God is perfect love. Is a good father interested in the problems of his children? Does he take time to remove a stone from a little one's shoe? To apply a Band-Aid, to fix a bicycle or doll, to help with the homework, to listen to troubles? If at all possible, he does. God, who is concerned about the business of running the universe, has time for the most trifling problems of those who are His children. A simple and sincere 'Our Father' will bring Him immediately to our side."

Where is heaven? Jesus said that the Kingdom of Heaven is within us.

Hallowed be Thy name. The opposite of hallowed is "profane"—and you cannot walk around the block these days without hearing someone, either consciously or unconsciously, profane the name of God. We are a blasphemous generation, and it must break the heart of God.

And "hallowing" means more than just *speaking;* we are guilty of blasphemy when we give God a divided allegiance; when we hold Him in disrespect; when we refuse to hold in high regard any other child of God than ourselves! *All life must be hallowed, for God created it.* . . .

Thy Kingdom come. When? How? Some of us seem to be praying, "Thy Kingdom come—but not just yet! I have some things to do, and do *my* way, before it comes!" . . . Let's get it straight. God's Kingdom is absolute. There is none other beside God. When we sing "My country, 'tis of Thee," the most marvelous part of the song, to me, is that which says, "Protect us by Thy might, great God, our King." Who can question His Kingship, or prevent the coming of His Kingdom? . . .

When we consider that in that day the lion shall lie down with the lamb—well, that will be truly heaven, will it not? No more tears, no more sickness, no more death, no more separation, hunger or thirst. That will be the Kingdom "come."

Thy will be done. . . . We'd better accept it: His will certainly *will* be done, whatever *we* do. God has the last word on earth and in heaven. When Lucifer and his unholy band of angels dared challenge the sovereignty of God, they were banished from heaven.

God also has the last word on the earth today. In the natural world we see natural law transcended by His Spirit. His will is done. . . .

How can we know the mind and will of God? How can we know His plan for our daily lives? Deciding about that is most difficult, as all important decisions are difficult.

I think the best way to arrive at the right decision is to first pray about it, placing it in God's hands. Then sleep on it. The next morning, when you get up, I believe that the first solution that comes to your mind will be the right one—that is, if you have complete confidence in God's guidance. "But let him ask in faith, nothing wavering. For he that wavereth is like a wave of the sea driven with the wind and tossed" (JAMES 1:6). Ask God's help in faith, and your decision will be right. I have found it unwise to make important decisions at the end of the day, when we are weary and tired. But once we have made a decision, we must not look back, like Lot's wife. We must act then on the faith that God has given us the answer —and know that only good will come out of it.

Give us this day our daily bread. Notice that God does not say "tomorrow's bread." We are not to be concerned about tomorrow—only about today. What is bread? In the deepest sense, bread is Jesus Christ.

Bread is sustenance. Jesus sustains us. He is our Manna, our Water of Life. Bread! Our bodies can fast awhile and deny themselves bread, with no ill effect, but when the soul goes on a fast, look out! We need the bread of Christ in our souls every day.

And forgive us our debts, as we forgive our debtors. Jesus says that unless we forgive others, we cannot expect God to forgive us. And it means something more than debts in money. Matthew uses the word "debts"; Luke says, "Forgive us our *sins*"; some of us say "trespasses," as the Episcopal *Book of Common Prayer* and the Coverdale translation have it, but all three words count up to the same thing.

So we had better forgive others . . . and we haven't really forgiven until we have forgotten.

And lead us not into temptation. . . . I don't believe that the Lord leads us into temptation; I *do* believe . . . that God allows Satan to tempt us, and for a good purpose. . . . I think it is reasonable to think that Christ means here, "Protect us from *yielding* to temptation. . . ." God allows us to be tempted as a test of our strength in refusing to yield to the temptation. And only God can give us the strength to keep from yielding.

He is ready and willing to deliver us from evil, if we want to be delivered. . . .

For thine is the kingdom. . . . It is interesting that these words were first spoken by King David, in I CHRONICLES 29:11: "Thine, O Lord, is . . . the power, and the glory, . . . thine is the kingdom, . . . and thou art exalted as head above all." David had quite an interest in kingdoms; he built a good one of his own—but he knew it was a trifling kingdom compared with God's. "The earth is the Lord's, and the fulness thereof . . ." (PSALMS 24:1). "He holds the whole world in His hands." He holds the earth, the other planets and stars, He holds space in His hands. Where would be the awe, the mystery, and the majesty of the great ultimate power behind the universe if we could completely understand this great God of ours? If I could completely understand Him, I might get tired of Him. Some people want to put God in a test tube. There just isn't a test tube big enough.

. . . *the power and the glory.* . . . Power! Imagine the Power that created the whole universe! Go out at night and just look up at the stars, at the countless galaxies swinging in the sky, and you will *feel* that power! Only God could have thought of it, only God could have done it.

When Commander Frank Borman and his fellow astronauts were in celestial orbit, millions of us heard

him say, "God created the heaven and the earth . . ."
(GENESIS 1:1).

God is *all* of science. He is all-knowing, all-under-
standing, all-powerful—and all love.

Let us never forget that we are absolutely nothing
without God. Said Jesus, ". . . without me, ye can do
nothing" (JOHN 15:5).

We have belonged to many churches since we came
to the Lord in 1948. I surrendered my life to Him in
the Fountain Avenue Baptist Church in Hollywood.
(I had already accepted Him as Saviour in the First
Baptist Church of Osceola, Arkansas, at age ten, and
was baptized by immersion at that time.) Roy was
baptized three weeks after he accepted Christ, shortly
before Easter, 1948, also at the Fountain Avenue
Baptist Church. Our children have been christened,
baptized and active in various churches: Chapel in the
Canyon in Canoga Park, California; St. Nicholas Episcopal Church in Encino; the Central Baptist Church
of Italy, of Italy, Texas; Church of the Valley, Pres-
byterian, in Apple Valley; High Desert Baptist Church

in Victorville; Chatsworth Methodist Church. Three of them gave their hearts to Christ at a Billy Graham Crusade in Los Angeles.

Wherever the Gospel of Jesus Christ is preached, we feel at home, regardless of the name out front.

Christians in the church are the body of Christ. We are His earthly eyes, shoulders, arms, torso, legs, feet— Who can say which part is best? Do they not all make up the whole body?

Christian love will solve our race problem. I do not know why God made some people brown, and some black, yellow, red, or white, and it's not for me to question Him, but to be glad for the variety he has given us in humanity. What a dull world this would be if we were all exactly alike! But, mind you, He has made the same moon and the same seasons for all of us. The blood runs red in all of us. The same Spirit is in all of us. We are *all* living souls for whom Christ died.

I also believe that in our free America everyone should enjoy an equality of opportunity. Every person who lives decently and works hard should be allowed

to attain his goal, regardless of race, creed, or color. I
certainly believe that every citizen who is of proper
age, who can read and write and carry out the duties
of citizenship, should be allowed to vote, for American
government is representative of all the people, and
they should all be represented in the government.

I do not believe that *social* acceptance can be legis-
lated or enforced by law. All of us must *earn* acceptance, respect, and friendship. It is a difficult process.
Some people just don't take to other people, even within the same race. But I think they should have the
same chance to live well. I think it was Bishop Paul
Hardin of the Methodist Church who tells of how he
played as a young white boy in the South with a
black boy. Both, in their first childhood aspirations,
wanted to be engineers on the big locomotives that
ran through their town. The Bishop, as a grown man,
got the chance to sit in a locomotive cab and run the
engine down the track past the very place where he
and black Jim used to watch the big iron monsters
go by, and he says he had a strange thought as he sat
there with his hand on the throttle. He said he realized
that *he* could be an engineer, if he wanted to—but that
Jim could not, for the simple ghastly reason that Jim
happened to be black and not white. See what I mean?
I think that wrong, and un-Christian—and so does

Bishop Hardin. We whites must extend ourselves in understanding helpfulness to our black brothers and sisters. They can learn from us and we can learn from them. . . .

We are all brothers and sisters in Christ; through Him, we are all the adopted children of God. This may sound involved, but I believe it. We are often called "an international family," and I see nothing strange or impossible about that. Wasn't the world made by one Father?

. . . Love—God's love—never fails. It may take a little time, but love will win, for love is constructive in its compassion: it lifts!

I found a living, leading Shepherd in the Twenty-Third Psalm.

According to this Psalm, He is a most intelligent and competent Shepherd. He is big enough to lead the *whole flock*, and yet He knows my name! "He calleth his own sheep by name. . . ." The Lord is *my* Shepherd. He stays with me through good and bad. Once He laid down His life for one lost Dale Evans who had wandered away from Him and His fold. I sleep in peace since He found me and brought me back, secure in the knowledge that He has given His angels charge over me. When my mind is stayed on Him, even in the most trying hours, my mind is at perfect peace.

"I shall not want," to me, means "I shall not *need.*" The Shepherd has met every need of my life. "For he satisfieth the longing soul, and filleth the hungry soul with goodness."

As I walk His way with this satisfied singing soul, all around me seems to be singing too. It is a blessed, happy walk, and I enjoy it as a sheep would enjoy being turned loose in a good green pasture to enjoy food and rest. I came to Him and He gave me rest; I know a calm spirit now that I never knew in my old world of conflict and suspicion and insecurity. I know His serenity. I can rest in the midst of uproar. I can look up at the face of the Shepherd and be quiet anywhere. I can be still and know that He is God. At night I claim His promise, "He giveth his beloved sleep. . . ," and I *sleep*—whatever happened today or whatever is about to happen tomorrow. I sit and watch His spirit moving in the gentle motion of a flower in the wind, in a tree that "lifts its leafy arms to pray," in the riot of color in a sunset, in the endless tireless surging of an ocean tide; I see Him in all this, I see His footsteps everywhere and I get up to walk again with a new strength. I love to "lift up mine eyes unto the hills," for on a thousand hills I see the Shepherd with His sheep. . . .

And He often leads me beside a quite lake [the still waters] and gives me healing there. "He leadeth me in the paths of righteousness for his name's sake." I have not always understood His leading. As a full-grown ewe sheep, when I asked Him to take my life and use it, He took me seriously and started to lead. He set my feet in wider and wider paths of service. I didn't deserve it, but I am grateful. Many times He has let me suffer illness or some personal setback; looking back at it now, I know how much I needed it, every time it came. I deserved it for I was trying to rush out ahead of Him—doing things on my own authority or "under my own steam"—not talking it over with Him, not following His map. I needed His restraint. . . .

If we enlist under Christ's banner and call ourselves Christians, He is not going to let us willfully dishonor His name without chastising us for it. For His name's sake, He will keep knocking us down until we get the idea. He says that if we are not corrected, we have no right to call ourselves the sons of God. He *forces* us into paths of righteousness for His name's sake, just as any shepherd would force his sheep to walk a safe path rather than one on which they might be hurt. He would *not* be a Good Shepherd, if He failed to do that. . . .

Even when I have been forced to walk in the valley of the shadow of death, I have learned not to be afraid. When our little girl died in 1952, the Lord showed me that He was there in the valley with me and that He had the whole situation well in hand, and asked only that I trust Him. Little Robin was unconscious most of the day she died. There were two nurses with her, and I was in and out of her room all day. She had encephalitis—brain fever—a complication which developed from mumps. Our doctor told us at noon that she was terribly ill and might not make it. I walked outside and a soft breeze fanned my face. I seemed to be in another world, and God was there. At four o'clock in the afternoon I went into the kitchen to prepare supper for the other children, and while I was doing it I suddenly knew that the Lord was going to take Robin home. I said aloud, "It's all right, Lord. She's Yours." Mind you, I adored this baby, and for two years I had fought to keep her alive.

At 7:45 I went in and kissed her good-by. Her breathing was labored. I turned and walked across the room; Lana, the big gray dog who loved Robin, was scratching furiously at the screen door and barking excitedly. Do dogs have a sense of approaching death? I know many people who believe they do. I walked down to the barn, praying and asking the Shepherd, "Please don't let her suffer any more. Please take her quickly." As I came back to the house Virginia, one of her nurses, met me and said quietly, "She's gone, Dale." Roy and I had a hard short cry, and then— peace. There seemed to be Someone Else with us. . . .

All through the next two days, all through the day of the funeral, the Shepherd was there. I had the feeling that Robin was there too, *that somehow it was all right,* and that it was best for all of us. The Shepherd never left us in the valley. I could never have walked through it without Him.

He has been there to help in other moments which at the time seemed almost as bad as death.

He has always prepared a new "table" in the presence of our—no, His—enemies.

He has anointed my head with the oil of healing, and my heart with the balm of happiness. As the oriental host poured sweet-smelling oil on the head of his guest, the Shepherd has welcomed me into His Kingdom with the oil of the Spirit; as the shepherd bathes the wounds of his sheep in oil, He has healed my wounds with His love.

The Shepherd has become the personification of

goodness and mercy, to me; He and they have been following me all the days of my life, and will always follow me. I speak not of my own goodness, but of His; it is His mercy that has forgiven me times without number and helped me up from my falling, to try again. He has known everything that has happened to me; He has anticipated every need, and provided for it all.

Everything around me seems so temporary. "Change and decay in all around I see." But the love and the mercy, the forgiveness and the kindness of the Lord hold steady and fast. I am never alone, never desolate. His goodness "faileth never."

"And I will dwell in the house of the Lord for *ever*." What a future that is! When career, home and children have come and gone, there is still the promise of Jesus the Good Shepherd, "Lo, I am with you. . . ."

This is my Shepherd, my Christ.

Ships coming into port slow down to "pick up the pilot"—to take aboard a man who knows every rock and sand bar in the harbor and who can steer the ship safely through them to the dock. When the ship leaves the harbor, the same pilot comes aboard to take her out to deep water and the open sea, and then they "drop the pilot."

"Dropping the pilot" has always made me sad, whether it happens on a ship or in a human life, but "picking up the pilot" always thrills me. "Jesus, Saviour, Pilot me," I sang as a child, and it means more to me now that I have put away childish things. I suppose I picked up and dropped a dozen pilots for my life's voyage, before He came to guide me. Don't we all? When the boy is six he wants to be a fireman; at ten he would be either a cowpuncher or president; at fifteen an astronaut, then a lawyer, doctor or minister. We all pick out our heroes and worship and imitate them—dream that we may be like them when we grow up. We'd save a lot of trouble and frustration if we would pick up Christ as our Pilot while we are still young. Why must we wait half a lifetime before taking Him aboard?

I say there is no better pilot, for He has been at it longer. He was here with the first of men and even before that; He said, "Before Abraham was, I am." He was here before Abraham was here. "For by him were all things created, that are in heaven, and that are in earth, visible and invisible, whether they be thrones, or dominions, or principalities, or powers: all things are created by him, and for him: And he is before all things, and by him all things consist" (COLOSSIANS 1:16–17). God in Christ *created* us; could you think of one better able to guide us?

Roy has a popular record of a country song entitled "Money Can't Buy Love." Aside from his fine job of singing it, the song says a mouthful—and a heartful. Money has never bought love between lovers or between parents and children. A five-dollar bill is a poor substitute for love and interest in a child. A fiver is soon spent, leaving the child still hungry for the satisfaction and security of knowing that his parents really care enough about him to get deeply involved with him.

My generation, in the wake of two world wars, has been guilty of not getting involved—enough. Many mothers had to work during wartime, and all too often they came home to a hungry daddy and children who needed them, and they refused to act like mothers and the keepers of the home fires. They preferred to work for the extra car, television, or mink coat, and by the time they had it, they didn't have much left for the family. Many a child grew up against a ground of no cookies and milk after school, and in real companionship with mother and father. We got a rebellious generation out of that—which was just what we deserved.

The hand that rocks the cradle can either wreck or rule the world. Are we bent on wrecking it, after all this time and experience? Of course, childbearing and child rearing is often hard, monotonous, and thankless. What isn't? I have worked as a career woman in the business world and in "show biz," and I can tell you that it becomes dreary and monotonous and almost unbearable, at times. You work a lifetime at a desk and then you retire—to what? To unbearable loneliness?

There are some mothers who are especially gifted for service in areas other than motherhood, and some may be happier working in those other areas, but by and large I have found the happiest women functioning in the role of mothers. Some women are forced to work, and they need the help of nurseries, but no child should be left in an impersonal children's institution an hour longer than necessary. I am not interested, here, in arguing the pros and cons of Women's Lib, nor in debating their principles—some of which are good (the earlier Lib movement which gave women

the vote was *very* good). I appreciate all this. But I am still convinced that there is something even more important than the right to vote, or the right to equal pay for equal work. I am pleading for an increased effort to hold our homes together for the sake of the little people. Who, in a state or a county or local nursery, will take time out to say to a frightened child, "God loves you; you do not need to be afraid"?

A well-known TV personality, interviewing me when we published our *Dearest Debbie* book, said something like this: "You know, when you adopt children as you and Roy have done, you just might be *asking* for troubles and heartache. Of course, you can have that with your own children, but when you go out of your way to take in other children, you are, more or less, asking for it, aren't you?"

She had something there—some of the truth, but not all of it. A tree extends its branches and grows in grace and beauty and strength when it strikes its roots down deeper, in standing against the winds and the storms that beat upon it. The same thing happens to us human beings. We are strengthened when, doing our best for our natural children, we see them grow "in wisdom and stature, and in favour with God and man" (LUKE 2:52). Roy and I have been strengthened even more in doing our best for those who, through no fault of their own, would never know the love of a home and a family unless we brought it to them—even though sometimes it ends in a tragedy that we cannot understand. *We live and we grow as we give.* God asks us to go the *second* mile. When we know how far Christ went for us, a mere second mile doesn't seem too much.

I think there is something inherently public in the word *witnessing.* What right has any man or woman to keep his faith strictly private?

Today, with Dr. Norman Vincent Peale and our publishers, we discussed the problem of publishing religious books, of how hard it is to get a book that will find any audience at all, with people in the churches so divided and quarreling among themselves. I think I'd rather write books than publish them, for the publishers seem to be sitting on a keg of dynamite that never quite goes off, but that just *could* go off at any minute.

Dr. Peale has the answer, I think. He says, "Write what God gives you to write, and forward all the letters of criticism to Him." That makes good sense to me.

I don't think I shall ever try to please anyone but Him. I think He would detest any other kind of writing!

When I was a little girl, the word *Christmas* was magic. It still is, now that I've passed thirty-nine (!).

Sometimes, when I was still a child, Christmas came for me in the summer, when we visited my father's folks in Mississippi. There I found the warmth of family love. What a wonderful time we had in that old, rambling two-story white house in Centerville, Mississippi. There were beautiful "summer Christmas trees" on the front lawn, adorned with velvety white magnolia blossoms. I remember the heavily-loaded fig tree just outside our bedroom window, and how I reached out and touched it. This was Christmas, too, in our hearts, for there was an abundance of peace and love for God and each other.

I learned that Christmas could come on a summer's day. Christmas could come at *any* season, if that sense of love were strong in the family.

Have you ever stopped to think that our Lord came to earth as part of a family? He heartily approved of the family, as a social and spiritual unit. When we talk about the first Christmas, do we not always see the Holy Family in the humble manger? It couldn't be Christmas, without them there.

When we are careless about our family relationships, we are losing Christmas.

In February of 1969 Roy and I faced a press conference in Houston. Press conferences are always ordeals; you never know what questions the reporters are going to throw at you. At this conference, one of them said to us, "You two people seem to be almost unreal, as though you had suddenly appeared out of a cloud in the West. Tell me: is it hard to be thought of as 'goody two-shoes'?"

That set me back a bit, because never since God revealed my unworthiness to me in 1948 have I thought of myself as "good." I am certainly not good (even Jesus asked, in MATTHEW 19:17, "Why callest thou me good?") and if there is anything about me that is at all acceptable in that sense, it is strictly due to my faith in Jesus Christ. Whatever good I do, He does through me.

Roy and I have those moments which every man and woman have, when we are less Christian than we should be. I would be less than honest if I said there had never been any squalls in my Christian walk or in our marriage. There have been tempests— but our house is built on the Rock, and it has stood firm through every squall and storm. We have grown together in our faith, and growing is sometimes a painful process. But with it comes—has come to us— a quiet, inner joy in knowing that by the grace of God we have learned to accept ourselves and each other as God's children and creation. As human creatures we still make mistakes, but our God makes no mistakes. He makes no two of us alike, but He breathes His spirit into all of us.

I told all this to the interviewer at the press confer-

ence. I told him that we were like all men and women
—two humans struggling and looking hopefully
toward heaven.

I love our young people. On the whole, I think they
are courageous, brave, honest and intelligent—and too
often frustrated by too much permissiveness at the
hands of overmaterialistic parents. Even though we
do not always agree with them, the least we can do is
to *listen* to them. Wisdom does not begin and end with
parents; it is something that is passed down to them
from generation to generation. Sometimes the kids are
right and we are wrong. "Out of the mouth of babes
and sucklings," says the psalmist, "hast thou ordained
strength . . ." (PSALMS 8:2)—and wisdom. Their
world is hurtling into change after change—too fast—
and the young people are trying desperately to meet
the changes at their level of understanding. Beneath
their rock-and-roll flamboyance they have a surprising depth of understanding.

I believe in the squares among youth. I believe that
their faith in all that is good will outlast the ravings of
our loudmouthed, sophisticated rebels, unwashed and

irresponsible hippies, draft-card burners and sexual deviates. The squares are in the majority; the others are the lunatic fringe. They will pass, and be forgotten.

My generation doesn't have all the answers—and neither does the Now generation. But the Bible has them—the inspired Word of God has *His* answers. It provides for the Establishment *and* for youth. (Speaking of the Establishment, let's keep it clear that the adolescent of today, the young people of today, are the Establishment of tomorrow. That's why we should be sending them to the Bible *now* for answers to the questions they're asking.)

It begins in the home—in parent-and-child relationships. Children are to love and obey their parents *for God*. Parents are to love, serve, instruct and discipline their children *for God*—as caretakers of the children for God until they are ready to move out on their own.

I believe in my country. I simply *cannot* believe that God went to all the trouble of bringing the Pilgrims and other settlers to these shores and of guiding the building of the greatest democracy the world has ever seen, only to let it be destroyed. He created America for a purpose still to be worked out in a distant future. His one increasing purpose for this country must be and will be worked out in the dedicated lives of God-oriented Americans.

Just after our astronauts, Anders, Borman and Lovell, circuited the moon and read from up there a part of the creation story in Genesis, we took time out to salute and honor them during a show at the Astrodome. It was one of the great moments in the march of man and history—and the Bible was the only Book big enough to be read at that moment. God bless them for doing that! May we have the courage to stand by Him as the creator of our Republic, the courage and strength to work for it, fight for it, live for it and if necessary to die for it. That is the least we can do for God and country.

Some young people are leaving the church because of the hypocrisy they observe in the churchmen. We in the church plead guilty; we do have a lot of hypocrites hanging around—but do we have more than our share of them? You can find hypocrites among the lawyers and the doctors and the businessmen and even among the atheists. The church has no corner on hypocrisy. When a young man told Dwight L. Moody that he couldn't join a certain church because it was full of hypocrites, Moody replied, "You're right. We have some hypocrites. But come on in. There's always room for one more."

We parents, we older Christians, can correct this sad situation by showing that in our own lives Christ has been sufficient for our problems. When youth sees the parents meeting a crucial test with Christian faith and confidence, they will be impressed and not disgusted. They will not stay in church simply because we tell them to stay. They want a better reason than that, and if our lives are right with Christ they will have that reason.

The church isn't a social club; it is a combination school and hospital for the soul.

I just noticed, in a New York evening paper, that New York City heads the nation in coronary diseases. This is not surprising. One day as we sauntered down Fifth Avenue, I scanned the faces of the oncoming pedestrians. Very few were serene. People walk fast, drive fast, eat fast, sleep fast, think fast, work fast— and die fast. It's wonderful to see the open church doors along the avenue, through which the hurry-harried people may quietly slip in and cast their burdens upon Him who can and will give peace and rest in the midst of all this teeming activity.

Another thought came to me as I watched the pigeons in Central Park; they are not the most popular birds in the world, but they can be and often are a quieting benediction for many of us. I watched the people feed the birds and the birds feed the people with their exquisite relaxation—a two-way blessing.

Someone has told me that psychiatrists often tell nervous people to buy a cat and watch him relax; the cat is the most perfect relaxer there is, and they can do wonders for our nerves if we just *watch* them.

So God uses pigeons and cats to slow us down. God's psychiatry is really something, isn't it?

Some well-meaning Christians make gods out of the things they don't do—like smoking, gambling, dancing —but what about the sins of the disposition, the intents of the heart, the little, mean thoughts that no one knows about except God and ourselves?

Jesus said, "Judge not, that ye be not judged" (MATTHEW 7:1). As the Christian matures, he will put away childish things.

Dodie and I were flying to New York last fall; the weather was rather choppy and there was lightning in the southern sky. Dodie had never seen lightning before, and her large black eyes snapped with fearful curiosity. "Mama, what dat?" she asked, and I replied,

"Why, that's God's way of speaking to us, Dodie—He's flashing His light at the world to tell us that it might rain." She pondered this for a moment, her eyes glued on the dark sky. The lightning flashed again. Suddenly she called out in an uncertain little voice, "God?" She waited, and then, louder, "God?" Another wait—then "God! Answer me!"

By this time, nearby fellow passengers were struggling to hold back their laughter, but Dodie never saw that. She said to me, "Mama, sing 'Jesus Loves Me' real loud, so He can hear." The drone of the plane was loud, so I could oblige our child without disturbing the other passengers, and she was satisfied.

Actually we never quite outgrow the desire for audibly hearing God's voice, or for a physical presence that we can touch with our hands. It's like the child who said, "I want a God with a face!" That's the humanity in us, even when we know better. "By *faith* are ye justified . . ."—by faith in the unseen, to do that which is best for us.

Not long ago I received a letter from a confused teen-ager who said she couldn't seem to "get through to God" in her prayers. So many people write about that. The wonderful thing about prayer, however, is that we do not have to depend on our feeling, but on the promise Jesus made when He said that if we asked of the Father in His name, the prayer would be answered.

Now God is not a mail-order house, but He is our Father. We shouldn't order something from Him expecting Him to send us just the right size, color and price on a specified date. He will answer the order in His own good time, which is different from ours—and the answer may not be the answer we want or expect. But it will be the right answer for us. The Bible asks us what father, when his son asks for a fish, would give him a serpent? No, our Father gives us only what is good, because He loves us. Sometimes the gift-wrapping looks a bit strange to us, but the gift is always perfect. When we are in Eternity, we will probably be quite abashed when we see, with Him, "the end from the beginning," and we will readily understand and praise His wisdom in handling our earthly affairs. Jesus said, "He that hath ears to hear, let him hear" (MATTHEW 11:15). God is speaking to us constantly, if our spiritual eyes and ears are open to the wonders He performs constantly. Many things we look upon as coincidence are really God's superb timing.

As much as it hurts me to face it, I must: early this morning, driving across Laurel Canyon and thinking over the years that are gone, I realized suddenly that there isn't one of God's commandments that I haven't broken, in one way or another—either by act, thought, or spoken word. That's a pretty terrible record. I wonder what my earthly father would have thought if I had deliberately set out to disobey every order he ever gave me? I got spanked, as a child, for disobeying only a *few;* I hate to think of the punishment I deserve from You!

How merciful you are, Father. How much You must love us. It is too much for me to understand, too much for my little mind to grasp. It is overwhelming for me to think of how God gave Himself in His Son to this wayward and perverse and unbelieving civilization, as the supreme sacrifice on His altar of love, to redeem our souls. We certainly don't deserve it.

I don't understand it, but I believe it. I see things dimly now, Father—as through a glass, darkly; it strengthens my faith tremendously to know that one day I shall see clearly, face to face. . . .